Strong Feather

STRONG FEATHER

POEMS BY
Jennifer Reeser

ABLE MUSE PRESS

Able Muse Press

www.ablemusepress.com

Library of Congress Cataloging-in-Publication Data

Names: Reeser, Jennifer, 1968- author.
Title: Strong feather : poems / by Jennifer Reeser.
Description: San Jose, CA : Able Muse Press, 2023.
Identifiers: LCCN 2020057224 (print) | LCCN 2020057225 (ebook) | ISBN
   9781773490885 (paperback) | ISBN 9781773490892 (ebook)
Subjects: LCSH: Indians of North America--Poetry. | LCGFT: Poetry.
Classification: LCC PS3618.E443 S76 2021 (print) | LCC PS3618.E443
   (ebook) | DDC 811/.6--dc23
LC record available at https://lccn.loc.gov/2020057224
LC ebook record available at https://lccn.loc.gov/2020057225

Printed in the United States of America

Cover image: *Koon-za-ya-me, Female War Eagle* by George Catlin,
   1985.66.528, Smithsonian American Art Museum

Cover & book design by Alexander Pepple

Able Muse Press is an imprint of *Able Muse: A Review of Poetry, Prose & Art*—at
   www.ablemuse.com

Able Muse Press
467 Saratoga Avenue #602
San Jose, CA 95129

For my sister,

Melissa "Bee" Byrd

Acknowledgments

Grateful acknowledgment is made to the editors of the following publications in which these poems, or earlier versions, first appeared:

The Agonist: "Cherokee County Tornado Warning" and "Chief Timucua Answers de Soto, 1540"

Better Than Starbucks: "Battle of the Little Shell," "On an Observation by Yeats," and "Ritual Journey to Native America"

Choice Words (Annie Finch, editor): "Remembering How My Native American Grandfather Told Me a Pregnant Woman Swallowed Watermelon Seeds"

Expansive Poetry: "Ballade of Drowned Western Art," "Logan's Lament," "The Native Strain," "Sedna," "The Shame Totem," "Some Other Indians," and "To the Snakeskin on My Path"

First Things: "Matthew 10:42," "One Brother Suffers," and "You Raised a Missionary"

IthacaLit: "Not Mary," "Our Kind," and "White Lady"

LIGHT: "As Natives Go," "Baby Eats Buffalo," and "Taking the Snake Venom"

Literary Matters: "Regarding Russell and Remington" and "The Sun Speaks of Her Lover"

Love Affairs at the Villa Nelle (Marilyn Taylor, editor): "Villanelle on a Line by Plenty-Coups"

National Review: "Cloud Bank Over Broken Arrow," "Disaster Relief," "If I Were Present at the Tribal Blessing," "Mission to Texas," "Strong Feather's Father," and "To the Dead Opossum"

The Polyglot (special issue by Indigenous contributors): "Nunda is the Sun" and "Quan'ta"

Rattle: "A Forensic Anthropologist Breaks Bad News to the Arapaho" (Poets Respond feature), "Formula for Frightening a Storm," and "Strong Feather Buries the White Woman"

San Diego Reader: "Bison Burgers and Fry Bread," "From Chilhowee Mountain," and "Reservation"

THINK: "Ode to My Silver Buffalo" and "Strong Feather"

Trinacria: "Formula to Fix the Affections"

Contents

Strong Feather

With the Waters

Sun and Fire

Up from Dust

Therefore, let our proportions for these wars
Be soon collected and all things thought upon
That may with reasonable swiftness add
More feathers to our wings.

—William Shakespeare
Henry V

Strong Feather

Against the Wind and Sky

Strong Feather

End of the winter, middle March,
Waking, I find it beneath my quilt
Clinging to linens the hue of larch,
Softer and whiter than milk when spilt—
One petite feather. Its hollow hilt,
Pointing toward me, is curved and long,
Slightly translucent, and at a tilt.
How has this feather stayed so strong?

Dainty enough to inscribe fine parch-
Ment, all through the night, without shame or guilt,
One fluid plume, as stiff as starch
Rests near the footboard an ironsmith built—
Brave as a lover I cannot jilt,
Diffident whether it's right or wrong.
All through the day it will stay, without wilt.
How has this feather stayed so strong?

Somehow unflinching, and yet not harsh,
Dropped from the crown of a crane or stilt
Wading in some indiscriminate marsh,
Rid of all filthiness now, grit and silt.
Bend to my question's quick, echoing lilt,

Grandfather Dashing Stream, Grandmother Song,
Draw near, reveal, dressed in heavenly gilt—
How has this feather stayed so strong?

Our Kind

Hair black as plumes around the roaming crows,
Flesh dark as copper kettle drums when burned,
My father brakes, decelerates, and slows
To stop for fuel, only to be spurned.
We do not serve your kind here, comes the warning,
From counters stocked with ten tobacco brands
By "Injun" names. I'm with him on this morning
In soul. I see the carved-wood chief which stands
Beside.
      Cigar-store statue, why remain—
Vice-salesman underneath a metal-signed
Injunction made against your very grain
Itself—a sad debauchery of "kind"?
Why linger at those exploitative doors
To scare my father's kind, and mine—and yours?

As Natives Go

I hear them speaking soft and low,
On Sunday morning after prayer,
You're really nice, as Natives go.

They mean the very best, although
I see a nervous hint, I swear.
I hear them speaking, soft and low.

I carry neither adze nor bow.
The statement arrows through the air.
You're really nice, as Natives go.

Upon my lifted hand, no crow
Affixes them with his grim stare.
I hear them speaking, soft and low:

I'm partial to the Sioux, you know.
Have you a near relation there?
You're really nice, as Natives go.

I see your skirt is Navajo.
My wife loves those fringe boots you wear.
I hear them speaking, soft and low,
You're really nice, as Natives go.

Strong Feather Buries the White Woman

As I unload each shifting, fertile clod
Upon her pale remains, their thudding sound
Brings to mind the pounding of that sod
Upon my mother's final resting ground.
Mother Earth, obliging, falls apart
For me. I see, instead of her I bested,
That *sweet*, blond thief who broke my mother's heart,
The one whom—all my life—I have detested.
What were the odds, that I could shoot ahead
Of her, this daughter of the Nordic gods?
This educated harlot once struck dread
Within me—puzzlingly. What were the odds?
If I can leave the thrill of her foul mouth
Filled with my mother's milk, I shall move south . . .

Ritual Journey to Native America

So summer closes. Now we travel north
To Oklahoma, where they found black gold
On Uncle's land. I'm twelve years old, and seated
Behind him, at the back of his red Mustang,
While cousins laze and sing "99 Bottles
Of Beer" to help improve my backward counting.

My cousins laugh, for they are going home
To Indian Country, leaving my loved bayous,
Returning to their clan another year.
The hot night wind whips hair into my eyes,
So I'm stung blind by tears—or so I tell them.
Have I brought with me Uncle's Native dolls?
I can't recall. The Mustang roughly rocks.
These shocks, as I sit settled at its rear,
Seem de rigueur for such an expedition,
As do the teardrops shed at my "removal."

For years, I shall not understand their joy,
Returning to that tribal territory,
Till Tulsa—like a hideout—is my home,
Where I will find my everlasting love,
And where my half-blood, first son will be born
Where I will feel that bond and that relief
In glimpsing everywhere an agnate face.

Familiar names I know and recognize:
Coushatta and the fierce *Atakapas*—
Although notorious for eating men—
I do not fear. The first beloved eyes
I ever saw in life were Indian.
But Tonkawa and Creek are strange to me
And frightening—whatever they consume.
I shift and ask my cousins to make room.

Disaster Relief

Three cuts I've gotten from the box knife's blade,
And needlessly, I wonder, "Will they heal?"
As we remove debris for those who stayed.
My last guess in the word game is "unreal,"
For this is not the way my thinking goes,
And these are not the ruins of my nation,
With certainty—this rubble from the blows
Of wind, these Sheetrock walls, this insulation
So sodden still, the flood soaks through my shoes.

Again, I stanch these cuts' rewelling blood.
My new shamanic name should be "She-Whose-
Feet-Are-Wetted-with-the-Tempest's-Flood."

I'm punching through, I'm kicking at the plaster.
My crewmen pity me, and interfere—
Our common hope, to mitigate disaster.
No tear they'll see, no outcry will they hear.

These walls of heavy paper we must gut
And haul away, with dust mask on, and glove
To insulate our fingers as they cut
A horizontal channel just above
My chest height, for removal—water stained
These nursery murals, adding to the anguish
That not one wall evaded and remained.
Their hues, already muted, further languish.

Like skeletons of steel, the studs are shown
While kneeling women, wielding power drills,
Evacuate the screws. Each sterling bone,
As we look out beneath our ball caps' bills,
Gleams glamorously. Flecks of silver glitter
Cover me, from some child's plaything smashed
When Harvey made his landfall, drunk and bitter.

I think the guardian cherubim of glamour
Must have a sense of humor, so to dress
Me now in tinsel, gaudy and yet tender.

My demolition team persists to hammer
And hustle through the hallways, through the mess.
The angels sprinkle them, as well, with splendor.

For My Son near the Coronavirus Outbreak

As I burn sage the proven, proper way,
    To purge the air by proxy, distant son,
Show prudence. You prepare and I shall pray.

Let pathogens be gone; this prolix day
    Be borne away—red flags, seared by white sun—
As I burn sage the proven, proper way.

Cleared is that wind through which you breathe; that clay
    Is cleansed, though Wuhan breaks into a run.
Show prudence. You prepare and I shall pray.

Though quarantines in Hubei province may
    Prove moot, you are protected, precious one,
As I burn sage the proven, proper way.

Its charring is, for me, like child's play—
    Sure ceremony, shut soon as begun.
Show prudence. You prepare and I shall pray.

And though they price the masks to profit, they
    Delay prescription from a vaccine gun,
As I burn sage the proven, proper way,
Show prudence. You prepare and I shall pray.

Formula for Frightening a Storm

An Ancient Cherokee Shaman's Formula Translated

Ha! Listen! Now, you're coming into rut,
And I am vastly apprehensive but
You follow on the course your wife takes, merely.
And I have pointed out her footsteps clearly.
Observe them going upward to the sky.
The paths, in your possession there, will lie
Without disturbance. Let your passage seize
The lofty mountains, and the tops of trees.
Listen! Let your walkways, as they go
Along, meet where the waving branches blow.

Chief Timucua Answers de Soto, 1540

In years past, others cursed among your race
Have brought their poison to our peaceful shores.
They taught me what you are. What's your employment?
To wander here and there, like vagabonds
From land to land, to rob the poor, betray
Confiding souls, to murder in cold blood
Defenseless ones. No! I desire no peace
With such a people, no companionship.
War! Never-ending war is all I ask.

You boast that you are valiant. This may be,
But no less brave are my true warriors—
And this, too, you shall one day validate,
For I have sworn to keep unsparing conflict
While one white man remains within my borders,
Not only in the fight, though even thus,
We do not fear to meet you, but by ambush,
Surprise at midnight, and by strategy.

I am a sovereign king in my own land,
And never will I turn into a vassal
Unto another mortal like myself.
Vile and pusillanimous is he
Who will submit unto another's yoke
When he may nonetheless continue free.
So, as for me, de Soto, and my people—
We choose death, yes! A hundred deaths, before
The dispossession of our liberty,
And subjugation of our native country.

Keep on, betrayers, thieves! From Apalachee
To Acuera, we will treat you as deserved,
And every captive we will draw and quarter,
And hang from the highest tree upon the road.

Cherokee County Tornado Warning

I sense the storm
Five hundred miles away,
Though at my sister's call,
I do not answer.

To my discredit,
I neglect to pray
Before returning it
To ask of the danger.

Her laughter is oblivious—
The alert unheard
And thus, unheeded—
The laughter
Of an unconcerned,
Brave bird.

The tribe, she says,
Has sent her on a chase
Unto the Choctaw,
Who then referred her case
Unto the Muskogee/Creek,
And back to home once more.

No static as we speak.

She tells me plastic
Will destroy the planet.
And have I seen The Hostiles?
She's driven. Nothing drastic
Will drown me, though, this morning.
Distracting, she's sarcastic,
And I forget the warning.

Mission to Texas

Hurricane Harvey Aftermath, 2017

The drone of drills amid this constant clamor
Of deconstruction—screw and power saw,
Spoiled insulation piles the hue of straw
Ripped out with force, by crowbar or by hammer—
Is not without a certain epic glamour.
The noises leave my nerves harassed and raw.
This gutted room is like a gaping jaw
Through which relief is gained as stud guns stammer.
These Orange Texans ambushed by the rains
Of Mother Nature, at her cruelty's height—
These victims whom my crew has come to save—
Are blessed indeed. For not one mouth complains
Of all who risk themselves, to heal this site:
The cowboy, and the cleric, and the brave.

Strong Feather Reveals Herself

They told you I would come, and here I stand.
In doeskin, poorly covered, though well versed,
As prophesied, as preordained, as planned.

A bow upon my back, a pen in hand,
Perhaps not most exalted—but the first—
They told you I would come, and here I stand.

My blisters, as I shuffle through hot sand,
Are gruesome, but I neither starve nor thirst,
As prophesied, as preordained, as planned.

A woman!—independent and unmanned,
By Mother Nature birthed, by Nature nursed—
They told you I would come, and here I stand.

No Lamb of God am I, no Promised Land
Do I procure—but look! The storm clouds burst,
As prophesied, as preordained, as planned.

Descending fluff of doves drifts down, a band
Of rainbows shows as thunder is dispersed.
They told you I would come, and here I stand,
As prophesied, as preordained, as planned.

Parish of the Crying Eagle

He flies Louisiana's sunken heel
Above the crow's wind-driven, drunken course,
Surveying the undoubted-though-surreal,
The Crying Eagle—till his throat is hoarse.

Those cannibal Atakapas who roam
Through Calcasieu in realms of History,
Imprinting themselves yet upon my home
This hurricane has crushed—what do they see?

The rainfall rising fast to wet my chest—
A mere twelve inches more before my head
Is drowned—the River Calcasieu's new crest
Historic: records break its brackish bed.

He flies a fluid skyline, made nightmarish
With cyclones sending pin-and-needle pricks
Down to my fingertips, that blessed word, "parish,"
A threat of double meaning, soaked with tricks.

Battle of the Little Shell

The Little Shell survives with sticks
To start a night of politics
By striking on an elk-hide drum,
When every member waxes mum
Within a warehouse built of bricks.

They are survivors; ten plus six
Score years pass—years which fail to fix
Their landless lot. Yet overcome
They do. Alive and thriving kicks
    The Little Shell.

The "garbage Indians" who mix
In shanties—housed like lunatics—
Do not surrender, nor succumb.
Four generations hence, they hum
Ojibwe songs, and light late wicks—
    The Little Shell.

Slain Eagle's Spirit Speaks

Fourteen people appeared in court this month for their involvement in illegally trafficking eagles and other migratory birds. Authorities are still looking for another man facing the same charges. The appearances come after a two-year undercover operation by the U.S. Fish and Wildlife Service called Project Dakota Flyer.
    —Argus Leader, *May 16, 2017*

A dozen report to judicial court,
For Mercy is appalled:
It is illegal to murder an eagle,
If golden, or if bald.

With those who answer, a Buffalo dancer
Inhales, then holds his breath:
One man—no, two—Lakota Sioux
Indicted for my death.

As I fill with fury both judge and jury,
The journalists relaxed,
A few faces pale—a pathetic tale:
Head severed, talons axed.

Stuffing like rags into plastic bags
Meant for trash, but never the noble,
They divided me, who had flown so free
The airplane seems immobile.

No painted pony. No ceremony.
No women in vexation—
With tears—who tremble. Observe the symbol
Of liberty to a nation!

Undercover sting to avenge my wing,
These agents—by subterfuge,
Through fraudulent talk—apprehend a hawk,
By playing the paying stooge.

To myself, I think (with that slow, wide blink
Of the wounded, wizened bird):
Would the verdict come more deserved to some,
My testimony heard?

Shall I bring disease, to enshackled knees,
My assailants—scorning truce—
For my rightful pay, as the shamans say,
From Humanity's abuse?

"You Raised a Missionary"

For Max

At Louis Armstrong Airport, Jason takes
My black-clad arm as we approach the gates
Where no Saint Peter stands as guard, and slakes
My cheerlessness. The Czech Republic waits.
My son—the one departing—jokes, and makes
Me laugh through tears. "You raised a missionary,"
My husband says, and this despair abates.
Lord Jesus, on Your greater strength, I tarry.
How like Your fairer images he seems!
The blue eyes, blond hair past his ear in waves,
The goatee, like faint ash across his chin
Unshaved 'mid these evangelistic teams
Who long to raise Departures from their graves,
And save respected strangers from their sin.

Not Mary

One in three American Indian women have been raped or have experienced an attempted rape, according to the Justice Department. Their rate of sexual assault is more than twice the national average.
  —The New York Times, *May 22, 2012*

I see you, Mary, leaving the casino
At 1:00 a.m., you faithful Cherokee,
Your shift done—not in Vegas, nor in Reno,
But Tulsa, Oklahoma: tribal tree.
What *is* it, that this rare ethnicity
We share, should be so hunted, still, so marked
By every predator prowling near and far?
His cowboy hat pulled low, I see him parked—
As mine was—waiting in his red-skinned car,
Beneath approved Security's white light.
Sister of my sister—what we are
Is savages' distraction for a night.
"Hard Rock," we call it, we offended few.
No, Mary, no. Not this time, and not you.

Chief Powhatan to Captain John Smith, 1609

I now am growing old and soon must die,
Succession passed in order to my brothers—
Opitchapan, Catataugh, Opekankenough—
And next, to my two sisters, and their daughters.
I wish their seasoning could equal mine,
And that you loved us much as we love you.
Why should you take by force what's yours through love?
Why kill us, who provided you with food?
What profit, war? For we can hide provisions,
And fly into the forest, when you must,
By wronging friends, go hungry, consequently.
What is the substance of your jealousy?
You see we are unarmed, and predisposed
To fill your needs, when with a cordial manner
You come, and not with guns and swords, as though
Invading adversaries.
     I am not
So simple that I do not know it's better
To eat fine meat, lie well, and sleep in peace
Among my women and beside my children;
To laugh and to be merry with the English;
And, as their friend, have copper and have hatchets,
And whatsoever else I might desire,
Than it would be to fly from all of them,
Lie cold within the forest, feed on acorns,
The tree roots and such trash, to be so hunted
I cannot rest, nor take in food, nor sleep.
My men must watch, in such a situation,
And should one twig but break, all would cry out,
"Here comes their Captain Smith";
And so, in this sad way, end my sad life.

Thus, Captain Smith, this soon might be your fate
As well, through recklessness and indiscretion.
I therefore urge you to convention calmly.
Above all, I insist the guns and swords,
The motivation of our jealousy
And turmoil, be removed, and sent away.

From Air the Hound Appears

From spring gales, he emerges, to appear
A golden guard through morning's solar prism,
A sunlit guide of canine mysticism,
Unleashed and fearless, warmly drawing near.

His presence is enough to cause a stir
Among the neighbors going door to door,
Who say they've never seen him here before.
He watches me, and thinks, "I'll follow her . . ."

Observing how I scuff the curb, he launches
Himself upon the pathway I have crossed.
"Not all who wander," I am told, "are lost."
White forelegs, muzzle, underbelly, haunches,

And tail suggest a phantom's subtle coat.
No plate identifying him, nor tags
Do I turn up on touching, though there sags
Black webbing for a collar at his throat.

Coming to heel, he paces with me, stops
To wait, until we reach the intersection—
Ears pricked, alert, as though I need protection—
Then vanishes behind a side street copse.

He seems to sense my travels reach their end,
And I—the wilder creature here—must be
Allowed, without a friend, to wander free;
That we agree, I am not his to tend.

My vigilant, attentive, spirit hound—
To whose unguarded journey have you gone?
Whose miles and miles are you now focused on?
And what adventure further have you found?

To the Dead Opossum, as I Take Her Baby
to Heckhaven

Poor mother, murdered by our human error,
Iconic in your windswept roadway grave,
More grievous for your orphaned daughter's terror,
Not understanding I have come to save.
Beneath you clinging still—untold, unsure—
I shall not leave her, destined like some tortoise
Or shattered armadillo. Premature,
It seems, this late phase of your rigor mortis;
Unfair, how far your flesh has come to harden.
No second Eve am I. Trust her to me.
The first time, you were murdered in the Garden
Of Eden. Commend me, by your memory.
I feel you watching from that Final Wild.
I hear you: "Prosper, She-Who-Freed-My-Child."

Evading the Black Snake Firm

The Black Snake Firm defiles and follows,
In search of me, yet fails to track
My whereabouts—for swifts and swallows
Have swabbed my path. A ghost wolf pack
Directs me to the next hotel
Where I adopt fictitious names
To harbor me from Summons Hell
And their supreme, but evil, aims.

But, Justice! Know me, recognize
For what it is, the serpent's hiss,
And clear me of its claims—likewise,
Deny them time to chase, dismiss
Their salivating allegation;

For I cannot forever trudge
From tribe to tribe, nation to nation,
With innocence, alone, as judge.

Dream of a Dying Hummingbird

The dimness felt in dream could not relieve
My grief, to find that hole torn in its breast.
What guides of thought and conscience, though, conceive
This test for me, nocturnally expressed?

On waking up, I can no more recall
Its color, nor its name (but maybe "Flower"?).
Only how unfortunately small
It was; how faint, in fortitude and power.

And that it seemed so keenly I was robbed
Of something irreplaceable—a trust
Lost for all time and likeness. So I sobbed
With that fierce force we save for the unjust.

Still as I say this, one can hear those cries,
So yawning is the memory, so fresh,
So deep, the senselessness of its demise,
So helpless in my palm, that loyal flesh.

Beside a darkened corner stood a shelf
Of books, where one had fallen, bafflingly.
The bird flew down and sacrificed itself,
Recklessly retrieving it for me.

Am I that hummingbird? Or have I lost
My truest friend and fondest pet this night?
And what was in those pages, that they cost
My unassuming treasure's tragic flight?

Faith in Perfection

Have faith in the perfection which is there.
Have faith, and do not let them beat you back,
Even if you must fade into thin air.
What slips their vision too, may they not track.
Who are they, after all? Fowls on a rafter
Which peck at crumbs, and to each other call
By common sounds, in love with their own laughter
Above you—but what *are* they, after all?
A fine fat falcon, polishing his feather,
Who ushers illness into human livers;
A pretty shrike who joins him, where together
They preen at table edge: Indian givers.
Ha! Now their shades dissolve against Belief,
And warmth comes, with immediate relief.

With the Waters

Ode to My Silver Buffalo

My silver buffalo, let me drink
So boundless from your depths, I think
The flavors of your fluids flow
Transparently as molten snow
Sprinkled beneath a mountain's brink.

Beside me, slake the baking pink
Adobe, where I lie and blink
In bright sun on this patio,
    My silver buffalo.

While meats are sizzling, ice cubes clink—
This crowd stiff as a skating rink—
From over the horizon, show
Me shafts of shoulder bones aglow,
On shamans brushed with india ink,
    My silver buffalo.

In Praise of My Osage Side

My father teases me
I cherish Cherokee
From Mother, holding his tribe's genes a ruin.

But what he doesn't know,
Because my key is low—
My pleasure in his blood of Osage Siouan.

As one of many daughters
To "People of Midwaters"
By name, mine is a pride no man can pierce,

Nor mortify through jibe.
I'm traced from that strong tribe
Of tallest, finest looking, and most fierce

Of any native race
Inhabiting this place,
Who thus established their authentic grounds.

These hard two thousand years
Beside the Trail of Tears,
My Osage half claims fame around those mounds,

Cahokia—where I
Climbed upward toward the sky
To find what Job and Moses must have found.

So, though my Cherokee
Is matrilineally
My truer tribe, by whose stock I was raised,

Let it be never said
That—selfish and ill-bred—
I left the Osage slighted or unpraised.

The River, the Traffic, the Scar

Enough time now has passed, my scar well crested
Into a river, elegant and white,
That—having been unquestionably tested—
I may accept this standpoint as my right.

A black elk by my side, I scrutinize
The landscape where no Long Man crosses over
With chuckling, liquid currents, froth for eyes,
Nor banks absorbed by Oklahoma clover.

Instead, by contrast, unrelenting graphic
Depictions of industrial pursuit
Ahead of me rush past, the morning traffic
Composed of quests—some distant, some acute.

Here are my scars, from mishaps of the past;
There is a river, undisturbed nearby;
There is this transportation, flowing fast
Before, horns fading to a muffled sigh.

And how I wind these things into a braid
Whose common symbol is the winding course
Long Person—River—takes, I am afraid
Escapes me, with the high wind's driving force.

Though I am home in Native land, it makes
no difference. The profiles so akin
To mine reflect me, as this people takes
the bus to businesses with thickened skin.

His head held high, majestic Black Elk stands.
With full cognition he remains supreme
Among the undiscovered forest lands,
His gaze fixed on these passengers' main stream.

Like Black Elk, I could linger, too—aloof,
Forged in a form of cooled and costly metals—
A pedestal of stone beneath my hoof,
Surveying Broken Arrow's prairie petals.

But Black Elk tells me, "Go," so I obey.
One values all the more the things one lacks,
And he would not acknowledge, anyway,
My strong desire to stop him in his tracks.

To My Granddaughter in Her Teepee

Standing stiff and straight as the poles that hold you,
Bear and cotton terrapin smooth beneath you,
Bare and tiny feet on the campground blanket—
Look at you, sweet one!

Alexandra, listen—repeat my greeting
While you balance perfectly, early dancer.
Go and give your father—my first-born treasure—
Something of value:

How the stars, like overhung fabric fireflies,
Glare and blink and flit in a patchwork pattern
Sky to creek, against an array of rainbow,
Daylight through darkness.

Little mimic, loyally miming Granny,
How your studied mimicry brings me comfort!
Your precise and serious repetition
Strengthens my being.

Now, you lean towards the mesh, sea-blue lining,
Though you clearly know the waves can't be trusted.
Clever child—already my graceful skeptic,
True to genetics.

Pines behind you, mountains embroidered under:
Hare, raccoon, fish, brook, sun, and bird above you—
These should surely love you, not a moment's
Feral misgiving.

Brother, You Bring Peace

Brother, you bring peace once more and balance,
With crystals, lilacs, butterflies, and phlox,
Your confident humility—that valance
By which the drapes of joy hang from a box.

Apache! Pull me up, then let us travel
Across the Native Holy Land together,
Our blankets not permitted to unravel,
Whatever we experience of weather.

And water down my fire, to reprieve
The serpent of control in me, and free
The doe you know and love. Let me believe
In your devotion and fidelity.

The Courrier du Bois and the Savage

Frederic Remington, 1891

Are these the forebears, clasping hands in trust,
   Of children pledged to peace—the one in fur,
The other nearly naked—safe from gust,
   Between these copses where no currents stir?
The lodged canoe, the lake below it placid
   As glass reflecting cautiousness with fog,
     Is put ashore too far for rapid flight.
   Between these figures, one can sense no acid
Nor caustic voice, nor does suspicion clog
     Their amity. So wise, the black and white—

Revealing no tone difference in the skin,
   But only depth, but only darkness, shades
Of charcoal to display the moods within,
   As one possesses, while the other trades.
Here, we will glimpse no jades preferring war
   To boredom, nor the reptile, nor the raven
     Like some crazed saxophonist in the brush
Who screeches that the poet is a bore,
   Or breaches all agreements in this haven
     Where no waves billow, and no whitecaps gush!

His arrows safe against his wiry flanks,
   The native's quiver fringe presents a match
To that the trader wears. The level banks
   Expose their equal height. The trader's hatch-
Et hangs—unheld—above his lowered gun.
   Assurance, frankness—let those words be spoken,

Not just in introspection, but aloud.
Coureur des Bois—Wildwood Runner—run
With confidence, this Indian no token,
No trophy, but a man, both meek and proud.

Shape-Shifter

They boast of loading weapons, to prepare
For my arrival through the hostile night,
When sentinels intensify their sight
On their objectives, difficulties, their
Predicaments, and too, place faith in prayer.
I grant them this. They may, of course, be right.
But where I crawled the forest floor, in flight,
Behind them like a dart, I now split air.
My structures ever liquid and so strange,
Move after angry move, for all their quick
And graceful wit, how shall they see me coming?
Man, so inflexible he cannot change!
Nor ever know the tactics to that trick
Of light, when drummers turn into their drumming.

Moving Out of the House

Gratefully placing my palm on the stairway, I thank it.
Instinct, with recall and soul, intertwines in an instant.
Out by the garden complains a dislocated gannet,
Croaking in answer to toads as though launching a bullet.

Porous, divorcing an era, I halt in the hallway,
Wondering how I will cope with the loss of this mainstay,
Going to Indian Oaks in the wintertime. Do they
Understand, those who are packing it up, in this mêlée?

See the house grieving with me, for the plumbing is leaking,
Suddenly bursts inexplicably; water, like weeping,
Dribbles in rhythmical droplets, which hit the hard tiling.
"Stop it," I say, wiping tears away, woefully smiling.

White Lady

White lady, in my dreams, you visit me,
Despite my hide of faded burgundy.

You welcome me to your marina mansion.
The butler leads me through its each expansion,

Then serves me tea—medicinal and sweet—
While parakeets, from swinging perches, tweet;

The room's resplendent with celestial light,
Its ceiling rising to celestial height,

Its colors and its feel, like cotton swaddle.
And you—so beautiful: God's supermodel,

Literate and merciful of face.
But why am I the ally you embrace?

I take it in, the custom-carved, clean nooks
In which reside obscure and classic books;

Your erudition, mild, athletic health,
And open admiration, when a wealth

Of low and lifted tones escapes your smile,
Reverberating off the marble tile.

I bite my tongue, in case I might be shunned,
As one might slight a global children's fund,

With "goody-two-shoes," scornful, pleading Audrey,
Or those who bolt away from tanned and tawdry—

White Lady, dear, fair friend: if I don't speak,
Forgive me. Wait another day or week.

And now, my faithful braves . . .

And now, my faithful braves are riding out
To put to shame my vicious enemy.
"His lips we shall cut off and hang about
Our flanks—and no more shall they threaten thee,
My love," insist these unrelenting men.

"Strong Feather, like the prophet-poet singer
You are, stand back, while—like the fierce Cheyenne—
We sever each extended middle finger
He shows to you and hang them round our throats
On necklaces we make from his dried bowel.
We'll leave him floating in wet petticoats
Sewn for women, while the wild wolves howl."

Great Spirit, who am I, that You should send
Devotion such as theirs, so deep, to cover
Me now? Not mother, daughter, wife, queen, friend,
Nor sister, goddess, shamaness, nor lover?

Strong Feather Colludes with the Sicilian

While I confer with you, his brutal foe,
Esteemed professor and most savvy scholar,
While lowering our heads, will you exchange
This wampum of my fathers for a dollar
If I lay down my arrow and my bow?

Our foe from "Washing Town"—though he may creep
About the choicer echelons—is still
Oblivious to my shark-minded sheep,
Knows not my summer name is "Niccolo."

The reputation is an easy kill
For one who plays the native piccolo,
To which both beast and genius bow their will.
But flautists will grow hungry, as they play.
Latin or Cree, we each have debts to pay.

Baby Eats Buffalo

Granddaughter, now at last you eat
Your first few bites of bison meat,

To grab it greedily—like a toy.
I can but barely mask my joy.

The peppers lying on your plate,
Both red and green, must lie and wait,

And likewise must the wholesome grains,
While you hunt something from the plains

Our forebears, for five thousand years,
Devoured with their cactus spears.

Then, between those dainty thumbs
And deft forefingers, lifting crumbs—

You cram them past your pretty lips,
Assault your sippy cup with sips,

And wisely gaze at me, as though
You knew about the buffalo,

As though the meaning in this meal
Sustains the hunger pangs you feel.

Smearing and smiling, might you guess
Its specialness and sacredness?

Like the Fishes

Those years of their mistreatment wash
Away, as though a rushing stream
In which the bashful fishes toss
About—creek chub with bluegill bream.

Their paths become a fractured gash
Of slivered sun between my feet,
To sparkle, stagger, drag and flash—
Sensational, and yet discreet.

They empathize so trustingly
With one who shares a quarry's troubles,
To peer with pain disgustedly
Upon my wounds through babbling bubbles.

All turns idyllic once again;
I swim in my romantic past—
My gills, a silver tunic, fin
Evading every angler's cast.

Taking the Snake Venom

I bite my tongue, then break
The tablet foil, and take
The venom of the snake—

This powder button bud
Which regulates my blood
Like placid drilling mud:

A viper from Brazil,
Contained within a pill
To cure my only ill.

What esoteric dreams
Will come from these blue streams
Of blood? What novel themes?

I tell my mellow man
Of medicine, it can
Enkindle and then fan

Such strangeness in the night!
He answers, "Good. Then light
The midnight oil—and write."

Bison Burgers and Fry Bread

For Jason

Among my people, here again I am,
Preparing to be welcomed to the feast.
The immigrant, you're in a flow, at least,
Leaned back, as though you do not give a damn—
Before us, bison, sweet potato-yam,
And fry bread, not the bloated loaf of yeast
Which you would be provided further east,
From family, with sauerkraut and ham.

Could I adore you any more? Black glasses
To screen your round, perceptive Dresden eye,
At last, you try my fry bread (no molasses),
Approving it with love—my German spy.
Our friendly female Wolf Clan server passes.
You tip her, reverent as at Versailles.

To Former Chief Byrd, as the Five Civilized
  Tribes Convene

Councilman Byrd, as you address each five
We recognize, each a "civilized" tribe,
Preserved and representative—alive—
What privilege, if a witness might inscribe
A column in remembrance of these days!
The podium avows your presence—you,
Full-hearted, -blooded focus of my praise—
The first among all Cherokee chieftains who
Would speak both tongues, and therefore could unite
Two cultures in himself, the red and white.

Like some true modern from the classic past,
"Forget the negatives. Let us unite,"
You say. "This is the first time, not the last.
Together, let us come. Let's make things right.
By sharing culture, sharing every way,
We will redo the history once done.
Through national uncertainty today,
We'll tell how our Creator makes us one,
The real story of how we came to be,"
Presenting them the Seal of Cherokee.

The ceremonies blessed by Chickasaw prayer,
A Stomp Dance starts, and while a tribesman passes,
I see Grandfather's chosen style of hair,
His profile, and the black frames of his glasses.
Finish the anthem, choir of the young—
For you've no precedent in history—
Half in the English, half the Native tongue.
Let it be sung, and do not look at me:
As he would be, so true to life and proud
Of our descent, I catch my breath aloud.

Ballade of Drowned Western Art

Stark Museum of Art, Orange, Texas

Where are Russell, Bierstadt, and Paul Kane
With Remington and Teichert and the rest?
Hung helplessly, have they been drowned by rain,
Our finest paintings from the Old Wild West?
And Dunton's *Talking at His Fluent Best*,
His close-knit bronco riders in a brush
Of grays, the Sioux child's beaded leather vest—
Were they immersed beneath the torrent's gush?

And where is John James Audubon's blue crane—
Above the flood, or swimming in unrest?
Do Couse's lovers, spoiled by water stain,
Irreparably float—the brave's bare chest
Against his Native maid, who, chastely dressed
In buckskin, holds her cheek, to hide a blush?
Against her modest form is he still pressed,
Or have their figures turned to swirling mush?

"Harvey," they have called this hurricane,
Whose currents cover cattle at its crest,
Like those on Teichert's watercolor plain.
What comfort have I—that museum's guest?
Were they protected while the streams progressed,
Like mines of gold to which those pokes would rush?
Have they survived, untouched somehow, and blessed—
As if Harvey was bluffing with four flush?

Chief! Do those proud indigenous remain,
Or—like their forebears—did they die, distressed
Within their truly innate safe domain,
Their hopeless cries—for pride's sake—unexpressed?

If I Were Present at the Tribal Blessing

For Melissa "Bee"

Had I been present when those pastors blessed
The Tahlequah tribe, my sister by my side,
I would have held her hand with left palm, dried
My wet cheek with the right—her joyous guest.
In Sunday best, she'd be so sweetly dressed,
Even the roses round her would have cried,
And closed their petals shamefully and died,
In hopes she would collect them, to be pressed
Within some cherished book upon her chair.
That luncheon over, and the leaders gone,
If she and I were privy to their prayer,
She, also, would have risen and withdrawn,
With powers from a reunited pair—
Half of a sorority whereupon
No Native grace is greater, anywhere.

The Comfort is the Tasks

The comfort is the tasks
That dampen days ahead
When we assume our masks
Repining for the dead;

Like billows to a buffer
Of hardened, hand-worked beads,
To buoy as we suffer,
And boost our innate needs,

Between the surface features—
In likenesses of bear
Or lean, barbaric creatures—
And all the grief we wear.

Our rounds of labor soften
That chafe-prone, tender space,
As we regard the coffin
Through eyeholes carved in place.

On an Observation by Yeats

No matter what one doubts one never doubts the faeries, for, as the man with the Mohawk Indian on his arm said to me, "they stand to reason."
—*W. B. Yeats*, The Celtic Twilight

The man with a Mohawk Indian tattooed
Upon one arm would doubtless call it treason—
Or, at the least, primordial and crude—
To doubt the faeries, for "they stand to reason."

The man with a Mohawk tattooed on his arm
May sneer at the idea of water horses,
Or fallen angels or a Hell to harm—
To place unwavering faith in faerie forces.

To Will Whitekiller upon His Promotion to
    Head of Tribal Gaming

Whitekiller! How I miss those distant days
When, through our busy marketplace, your name
Called across the open air could raise
Customer eyebrows—whittling, while it came,
Each client's pale cheeks when the violent phrase
Was voiced: an arrow, having struck its aim,
Those twilights underneath the Tulsa sun
Where cyclone rains, in rouge and copper, run.

Coercing memory, I see you, still,
Blood-streaked from throat to thigh, your knife in hand
Unpacking at a slab the morning's "kill"
Shipped coldly six hours west, from No Man's Land—
A "hunter" tamed, with introverted skill.
Now, clothed in silk and linen, there you stand,
Commander of the cards. Who knew then, Will,
These tribal trails, which neither of us planned?
Who knew then—you a butcher, I a scribe—
We each would prove so loyal to the tribe?

To the Last Cherokee Midwife

Bring me burr root syrup, Que-di,
  Brewed into a cherry tea.
As if you were a British lady,
  Bring me burr root syrup, Que-di.
Picked in thickets lush and shady,
  Midwife of the Cherokee,
Bring me burr root syrup, Que-di,
  Brewed into a cherry tea.

Matthew 10:42

St. Patron's School depends on your support
To clothe the Native children, care for, feed,
And minister affection of the sort
We understand all human beings need.

Enclosed in these white envelopes, please find
Dream catchers in a Popsicle array
Of shades, to rinse the nightmares from your mind,
Encouraging the sweeter scenes to stay.

Made in China—for child labor laws
Prohibit manufacture at cheap rates,
But we have found donations to our cause
Decrease without such gifts, within the States.

Along with it, accept this lovely pen
With which to write your generous relief.
The Lord reward you, ladies, gentlemen,
Restore your faith, and strengthen your belief.

One Brother Suffers

For My Sons

One brother suffers, and another brother—
And then a third—is standing by his side.
This is the surest sign to any mother
By which her sons can be identified.

Not eyes of blue that make a sibling's match
Nor cowlicked hair that sports the same brown curl,
Not that they all watch films with Cumberbatch
Nor that they each pursue the same good girl.

One brother has been singled out to suffer.
Here is a watermark the same womb bore them:
Two more arrive like angels—bigger, tougher.
And for this act of blood, all saints adore them.

Quan'ta

With one swift motion of her infant arm—
Her hazel eyes unquiet though remote—
She grips the pendant hanging round my throat,
As though she finds dry comfort in the charm:
Two silver feathers, shielding her from harm.
No more does her expression show alarm.
She clings—a coughing swimmer, kept afloat
In my embrace, while outside roars the storm.
Then, with her deft left hand, she grasps a strand
Of my long hair, as sleek and silver gray
As what her other holds. "*You understand,
Grandmother,*" her dark silence seems to say.
And I reply, "I know, I know, yes, *quan'ta,* Grand-
Daughter. *Quan'ta.* Hey-ya, hey-ya, hey."

Sedna, Mistress of the Underworld

The Eskimos recount from ancient lore
The tale of one without a loving wife.
An Inuit dwelling on a lonely shore
With daughter, Sedna, lived a quiet life.

The girl grew beautiful, till every youth
Attempted to obtain her for a spouse—
But Sedna, proud and vain, found all uncouth,
Refusing to forsake her father's house.

At last, upon the breaking of the ice
In spring, an esoteric seagull flew—
Skilled wings of silver gliding—to entice
Young Sedna, and a winning song, to woo.

Seducing not with song alone, but words,
The gull swooped towards the girl beguilingly:
"Into the territory of the birds,
Into my country, Sedna, come with me!

The finest leathers reinforce my tent.
Soft bearskins will enwrap you by the fire.
My fellow gulls will listen, make descent,
And bring you anything you might desire.

Their plumes shall fall in fine folds to your feet;
Your lamp shall never lack abundant oil;
Your bowl will never be in need of meat,
And you yourself shall never have to toil."

Not long could Sedna, so bewitched, withstand
Such wooing, sung by one to whom the feather
Came freely—so towards the seagull's land
They made their way, and entered it together.

Arriving after long and brutal travel,
Sedna rested, only to discover
His song had been a lie, and watch unravel
The lovely story promised by her lover.

Her home, not something any wife could wish
It were, was not of leather pelts, but pinned
In patchwork style, with skins of wretched fish,
Which gave free entryway to snow and wind.

Instead of downy reindeer hides, her bed
Was hard with walrus wool, and she must live
Not on rich, sweet venison, but instead,
On foul fish, which were all the birds would give.

Too soon she found her husband gull had lied.
Regretting, as she shivered with a pang
Of hunger in her gut, how foolish pride
Had spurned her Inuit suitors, then she sang,

"Aja. O my father, if you saw
How miserable I am, then you would come
Before the ice and snow beneath me thaw,
While I still sit within this fish tent, numb.

If you could see me in my present danger,
Across the sea by boat, we both would hurry
Away from these, who treat me like a stranger,
While round my bed, the flakes whirl in a flurry."

One year passed, and again, the sea was stirred
By warmer winds. Her lonely father came
To see the country of her lover bird,
And finding Sedna, heard her beg with shame,

"O my father, let me now return!
Hear the outrage done to me. I cringe
To be the teller of what you will learn."
And having heard, her father sought revenge.

The Inuit destroyed those who defiled
His daughter, brought them down from arctic air,
To leave them irremediably piled
Within that land which brought her such despair.

The other gulls, discovering the dead
(for whom they mourn and cry until this day),
They set out in pursuit of those who fled,
And found the two at sea, not far away.

Over the boat, they stirred upon the air
A heavy storm; within the ocean rose
Immense waves, threatening the helpless pair.
Her father, in this mortal peril, chose

To offer Sedna to the birds. He flung
Her overboard. Then, cruelly, he took
A sharp knife to her knuckles while she clung
To the boat's edge with a tight death grip, and shook.

Her fingers severed, first joints to the nails
Into the tempest tumbled, there transformed
Upon the froth. They turned to living whales,
The second joints, to ringed seals as it stormed.

Meantime, the seagulls—thinking she had perished—
Allowed the storm to cease. The father let
His daughter back into the boat. She nourished
A hatred for him, never to forget.

Bitter and deadly vengeance, then, she swore
Against the Inuit. Once they had stalled
Against her native and familiar shore,
In safety and composure, Sedna called

Her dogs, who waited for her in those lands
With loyalty, from winter till the thaw.
And Sedna set them on her father's hands
And feet, commanding them with spite to gnaw

Them off, once he had fallen into sleep.
He woke, and cursed himself, and her, and those
Who maimed him, when Earth opened in a deep
Pit, to swallow them, and then to close.

In Adlivun, both of them would reside,
That zone beneath the Heavens and the Green,
Where Sedna—wounded daughter, seagull's bride—
Is now the Underworld's eternal queen.

Sedna Sinks the *Scandies Rose*

"JUNEAU, Alaska (AP)—Five fishermen missing after a
crab boat sank in the frigid waters off Alaska were feared
dead after authorities called off a search for those working in
one of the most dangerous industries in the U.S."
  —Associated Press, *January 2, 2020*

"The boat had years of experience working the Alaska snow
crab and King crab harvests . . ."
  —The Seattle Times, *January 2, 2020*

Entangled in her hair, Alaskan crabs
Crawl cruelly, gleaming steam this New Year's Eve.
She summons beating waves. A shower stabs
The sharks like liquid spears. The whitecaps heave:

A fury on the Gulf, no finless squall;
The seven-hundred-pounder crab pots freeze.
Two hours till midnight comes their Mayday call,
But only they would dare these deadly seas.

And five lost lives, for Sedna's spite, unskiffed,
Descend relaxed to drape the ocean floor,
Two (Inuit?) alone allowed to drift,
Airlifted by a jayhawk craft to shore.

Insistent to ignore the icing warning,
Heroic hunters all, they surely proved
As Sedna rose from rest on New Year's morning,
Unruffled by their company, unmoved.

Gulls orbit Sutwik Island's eerie rocks.
Her hard, clawed pets within crustacean cages,
Each crab pot, sunk to safety, mutely mocks
Its capture, while above the weather rages.

Among the party, which of them could tell
His partners—parted evermore from home,
Untimely brought to Eskimos' wet Hell—
Its mistress wants the strong teeth of a comb?

To free the creatures from each seal-black tress
While overhead, her spout of water spins—
That she may welcome them with warmth, may bless
And cleanse these guilty trappers of their sins.

Sun and Fire

Cloud Bank over Broken Arrow

Rolling from silver-blue, round, powdered edges
Outside to in, overshadowing hedges

Etched on the daisy-buff fluff of the prairie,
See it appear, unashamedly airy!

Blocking the sun with one corner, impeding
Glare like a Sky Spirit's bended arm, speeding

In no way, but glimpsed from the interstate, level—
Muscular shoulder defying the Devil.

Cumulus Watcher, from Mingo Road, study—
Sober, long-suffering, crimson and ruddy,

Stoic, unmovable, brave, bronze, aloof—
How this dough rises on each vaulted roof.

Grandfather Sun, through the eyes of the East,
Watches, himself, while it bloats as with yeast.

Scan the horizon beneath it—a tunnel
Paler in hue, horizontal white funnel

Traveling under with sheep of its own,
Not to leave, billowed above it, alone,

Something so dignified, formal, and grand
Journeying forth to the Radiant Land.

Lowering windows to smell the aroma
Buffeting through my revered Oklahoma,

Cherokee County is spreading its fingers
Upward in praise. The Creator's light lingers!

Strong Feather to Her Cheyenne Love

You boast, "Oh, how she loves me, this young one
I court in secret, court in silence, court
When all the priests and dancers of the sun
Retire in gloom, and painted horses snort
Themselves to sleep!" Inside the turquoise room
Within the east wing was a golden calf
Born yesterday. I placed an eagle plume
Upon it. When you sing of us, you laugh.
My love, to you, seems just another jibe,
And—as you would at any moccasin game—
When white men bring wax cylinders, to transcribe
Our songs of love, you never speak my name,
But only mock and mock before the tribe,
And change the lyrics—never twice the same.

Blackjack Coushatta

His arms, tattooed from elbows up,
Raise firmly, as he goes for broke,
A half-drunk, buff casino cup,
And Camel cigarettes to smoke.

He jokes with us and hits his bid
As cat-eyed dealers nod "okay"—
Clearly a reservation kid
Who visits every Valentine's Day.

This year, it follows Mardi Gras,
When he claims gaming floors were packed.
I wonder if Atakapas
Were those his forebears once attacked.

A backward ball cap hides his hair,
And spectacles, his almond eyes—
Yet curling round him is an air,
Although compulsive, sharp and wise.

He's good, progressive though not rash.
Against a surely losing stand,
A player may recoup some cash
Back-betting on his savvy hand.

He says, without despair or blame,
"Predicting probability
Is what's required to win the game,
Not luck or chance." And we agree.

Coushatta War Pony

Revolving at the center of the grand casino floor,
Exalted on a dais 'mid the slot machines,
The gleaming metal motorcycle turns—a horse for war
Illuminated by dynamic, blazing screens.

Anyone may win the senseless, black, revolving mount
According to the elevated, lit marquee—
Given certain sourcing in the pay-and-play account—
Though, as the sign reminds you, fifty games are free.

For garnering rewards exceeding whole estates in dollars,
Congratulations, Tammie, from Louisiana!
For braving both executives and broke, nocturnal brawlers,
Congratulations, Caroline, from Texarkana!

If I should feel content with my initial "virgin's prize"
And cease to wager for the gain of two meek dinners,
And not pursue the Native's cornucopia with tries,
Deferring to the panoply of Texas winners,

Instead, inspecting Indians in three-piece business suits,
Preferring to appreciate this feat, then stop,
Examining these "warriors" in unscuffed cowboy boots,
Conversing with the waitresses and those who mop,

My reasoning is simple. My decidedness remains
To keep my wits about me, in this high romance,
Believing I might save, and bring you greater gains,
And that I'm lucky for you, in the game of chance.

Missionary to the Maya

For Jason

Beloved, when you left us for the mission
In Mexico—five children, dog, and spouse—
I lit a votive candle in the house,
In place of my magnanimous musician
Who could not leave the world in such condition,
Who could not leave a beggar with his louse.
Its flame became a solemn chore to douse,
Its lighting would become a new tradition.
I heard your father's sermons in my head.
Your sacrifice my goal, my dream, my bliss,
You went—the man supplanting me, instead.
I watched with awe, yet never told you this—
Who could not leave a homeless drunk to carve
His pleas in paint on roadside signs, and starve.

My Beating Bow

Here end my sad, inadequate demands
Upon your chaste, unpenetrated feeling.
I leave you, Cheyenne brave, to rutting, squealing,
And steer my mount toward other cold Badlands.

The way I take, no virgin understands
Who lies abed, afraid of blood and peeling
Within the soul, who gazes at the ceiling—
A heart enwrapped in corn husks, blistered hands.

Tomorrow on the hoarse horizon, my
Wild roan will move too slowly, and be shot
Out from beneath me, Man, when I will die.

But not before my beating bow has got
Relief for this frustration, waling, waling—
As lethal as my love was unavailing.

The Rebuke

The rebuke is fast and frightening,
    In a flash, misunderstood—
Like a timber struck by lightning,
    Ever after, sacred wood.

And the ordinary being
    Is reluctant to once more
Lay a finger on it, seeing
    Its mysterious allure.

For its ashes cause consumption,
    And its splinters—burned to coal—
Reinforce the athletes' gumption;
    In its paint, they reach their goal.

But to laymen, it is cruel,
    What survives the bolt's attack,
And you never use for fuel
    Its debris. Your skin would crack.

Strong Feather Declines to Defend Her Enemy

Forgive me, if I do not choose to plead
For your foul life, to change fate, as you beg,
But settle back, instead, and watch you bleed
Dispassionately—neither thwart nor egg
These warriors on. Christ keeps no tallies, true?
And He is near the heart of those in need?
Then Christ should have no problem saving you
From being burned in your own powder keg.
You've heard that Pocahontas saved John Smith,
Throwing across his body her young frame.
That tale of Pocahontas was a myth
Invented by a white man seeking fame,
Who prospered from a promise, broke his pact,
Then left us destitute—like you, in fact.

Strong Feather Covers Her Tracks

Would they not *kill* to know my whereabouts?
Their blundered shouts, one after one, resound.
The sweet gardenia glides its white perfume
Into a night of streaming, humid breezes
And drowns my human scent with surety,
As right as rain beads following the storm.
My footsteps dot the wood, invisible
As only humble things can be. The leaves
Direct me, as they've always done, like flares.
I hear my hunters clearly, beer and blades
In hand. The footprint brushes clean beneath
My own. Trap after trap they've set—so basic
A squirrel could circumvent them with finesse.
The tactics of a cat who toys with mice,
The strategies of sleaze and condescension.
If only they could hear me laugh at these!
Line after line, snare after snare they've laid,
As though I do not qualify as sentient,
Nor understand these low manipulations.
The moonlight shows so many. The Great Spirit
Shows me the rest through sober intuition.
One after one, they call, in groups or singly,
Who call me *savage*, call me *monster*, call
Me "love"—those are the trappers most cold-blooded,
And those the most rewarding to escape.
The least of all among them to be trusted:
The traitors who blend glory with their greed.
These predators can't hear me. Their own voices
Distract them from my movements, in an instant,
Directing them astray; they seem to hear

The things they want to hear, sounds always centered
Upon themselves, and this!—this is my secret.
I trust their evil egos to mislead them,
Their proud infatuations with their progress,
And seldom must I even lift a finger
Toward some trick, to watch them come to nothing.
They will not bring themselves to nose the ground.
Not one sign have I left them to believe.
Not one nod which the moon might magnify
With silver quickness, flashing in reflection.
No embers have I left, that they might brand
Me one more mark on those thick cowhide belts
Above their covered groins where senseless beaver
Attests to their indifferent cruelty.
I do it for the women and the children,
The dignified and honest braves—the tribe
Of truth. For, in the end, these rangers—liars
From birth, and cheats, and killers without conscience—
Do not possess the compass guiding me.
Their condemnation—truly—is deserved.

Logan's Lament

"I may challenge the whole orations of Demosthenes and Cicero, and of any more eminent orator, if Europe has furnished more eminent, to produce a single passage, superior to the speech of Logan, a Mingo chief, to Lord Dunmore, when governor of this state."
—*Thomas Jefferson,* Notes on the State of Virginia (1785)

I call on any white man now to say
If he has ever reached my cabin hungry,
When Logan has not furnished him with meat;
If he, at any time, came cold and naked,
When Logan failed to cover him with clothing.

Throughout the course of this enduring last
Bloody warfare, Logan has remained
Idly at home, an advocate for peace.
My adoration of the whites was such
That when I passed, my countrymen would point,
And say, "He is an ally of the White Man."
I even thought to make my place with you,
Except for the abuses of one man,
A colonel you call Cresap, who last spring
In cold blood, unprovoked, not even sparing
My wife and children, killed my kith and kin.

There runs no single droplet of my blood
Within the veins of any living creature.
And this has called on Logan for revenge.
I've sought it. I've killed many. I have glutted
My vengeance. For my country, I rejoice
Beneath the beacon glimmerings of peace.

But do not harbor any supposition
That mine is the festivity of fear.
Logan has not ever been fainthearted.
He turns not on his heel, to save his life.
To mourn for Logan, who remains? Not one.

The Sun Speaks of Her Lover

A Cherokee Myth

Alone, by darkness, and without a name,
My lover came to lie with me each night
But kept his fervent face so out of sight
I wondered from which tribe and clan he came.
So, with the ash of embers from my flame,
I brushed his cheek before his early flight.
Next day, I knew. He now lives far, in shame.
No longer are we ever found together.
So marked we are, we neither seek another.
Forgive me, that I gave my love too soon.
All Heaven stands between us since: the weather,
The warmth, the winds, and time. He is my brother,
That one the Principal People call the Moon.

Nunda Is the Sun

A Cherokee Retelling

Nunda is both Moon and Sun:
Nunda when the daylight dawns.
Nunda when it's done.

The Raven Mockers

Returning from the hunt by evening gloom,
A hunter found himself too far from home,
So toward an *asi* coming into sight
He wandered, seeking lodging for the night.
Discovering the house unoccupied,
He stretched himself upon the floor inside
Against a corner overcast in gloom,
Then heard a raven shriek outside the room.
A human being, old and thin as wire
Arrived and sat—unawares—by the fire.
Again, a raven's cry, a raucous knife,
Slivered the stillness. "That will be my wife
Who comes now," wheezed a bird's voice, foul and flat.
Then, in a woman entered, flapped, and sat.

The hidden hunter held his breath, distraught.
"Two Raven Mockers, doubtless!" the man thought,
And shivered—for his wise, foreseeing teachers
Had solemnly advised him of these creatures;
Most envied and most feared of any witch
Among the Cherokee—one who could switch
From human form to raven, flying in
The dwelling of the ill; old, withered, thin
They look, from adding lifetimes to their own,
Ripping the hearts of invalids through bone.
Remaining secretive, suffused by fear,
The hunter waited motionless, to hear
The husband ask his wedded crone, "What luck

Have you had for the night?" Her shrewish cluck
Came back, "Too many shamans at the door,
So . . . none. And you?" "What I went looking for,
I got," he spat. "There is no risk I'd fail,
But your luck always comes to no avail.
But here, take this—cook it and let us eat."

Soon, the young hunter caught the scent of meat
Sweeter than any other he had tasted,
As she built up the fire, skewered, and basted
The victual offered by her counterpart.
Then, peeping out, he saw a human heart
Atop those flames by which the Mockers basked.
"Who is in the corner there?" she asked.
"There's no one." "Yes, there is—I hear him snoring."
As though in sleep, upon the earthen flooring
He stirred, remaining mute with frightened poise.
To waken him, the old man made a noise
Around the fire—but still, he seemed to doze.
Without a sound, the Raven Mocker rose,
Approached, and shook him till he made him rise
Like dunces from deep dreams, and rub his eyes.
By now, with dawn beginning to appear,
The wife preparing breakfast, he could hear
Her weeping—for, of course, the woman knew
If any mortal ascertained their true
Identity, the truth through their mystique,
The Mocker would be dead within a week.

The hunter asked him why the woman cried.
"She feels abandoned. Several friends have died,"
The old man lied. The hunter ate his mush,

Departing—when he saw the old man rush
To catch him, with a gift of hand-worked bead.
The fine piece handed over, "There's no need
Repeating what you overheard last night,"
He said. "My wife and I—we always fight
That way." Beads held, resolving not to speak,
The hunter moved along, but at a creek,
He halted, throwing them into the water
Disgustedly. "Now let them, with the otter,
Remain." Then to his settlement, he went,
And told his tribe about the night he spent.
A party of their warriors departed
To kill the Raven Mockers—brave, truehearted.

Reaching the wattle-and-daub abode, at last,
They found the lifeless two. A week had passed
Since their identity had been discovered.
So, where two birds of evil dreams had hovered,
The warriors tore down lattice weave and frame,
Blazoned a fire, and left the house in flame.

The Shame Totem

Erected to commemorate a debt
Ignored or scorned by some important man,
It rose, reminding damages were yet
Unpaid, to burn both family and clan
The way they would each creature's vivid face
By wicked tools and patient fingers carved
Across the fragrant cedar, till disgrace
Surfaced in full before the justice-starved.

Petroleum spills demanding retribution,
Despised by all, and ordered by the courts
To be redressed for their rude, bold pollution;
Some presidential slight—these are the sorts
Of offense which this totem seeks to school,
That we might learn the artist's love of Duty
Upon what's called the Pole of Ridicule,
From cunning craftsmen, disciplined by Beauty.

Disfigure them in effigy. Invert
And fix them on wood staves, for all to see.
The skilled, creative ones whom they have hurt,
By Art acquire immortal dignity.

Strong Feather Sets a Snare

His vanity was what I laid for bait—
His haughty appetite for showing off;
And so he came, as hogs approach a trough,
Or like a restaurant critic to the plate.
What brute could curb the brewing urge to rate
My humble morsel, with his lofty scoff?
Look! There he hangs, who taught them Romanov!
About to snap my rope, with his great weight!
No ally to the hunted and oppressed
As he professed, no human with a heart,
But one whose fire stick kills the Crows for jest.
Yet see his liberal costume come apart—
His hatred and hypocrisy unfurled
Before the just Creator and the World.

Formula to Fix the Affections

An Ancient Cherokee Shaman's Formula Translated

Ha! Now as one both souls have come!
You are of the clan of Deer,
I am of the clan of Wolf,
A-Ya-A-S-Ta is your name
I take your flesh, and of it eat
I take your spit, and of it drink
I take your heart, and of it eat. . . .

Ha! Hear me. Now it happens that the souls have met,
Nevermore to leave each other, you have said
Above, O Ancient One, suspended by a thread.
Black Spider, you've descended by a span.
Black Spider, you've descended from the height.
Ayasta, she was christened, from the clan
Of Deer. You have wrapped her in your silken web—
There, where always coming into sight,
The people of the seven clans appear and leave,
There never was the feeling or the need to grieve.

Ha! Hear me. Now you cover her with loneliness,
Her eyes becoming fainter, weak, and colorless.
Her eyes on one alone have come to drape.
Whither may her soul escape?
Cause her as she goes along to sorrow,
Not only from this moment till tomorrow—
Let her be one whose trail may not be followed.
Let her aimless, wandering soul be swallowed
Within your web, and not break through its mesh design.
What's the soul's name? They're uniting. It is mine.

Ha! Hear me. And now take note, O Ancient Red,
O Fire, and your children's children now are led
Unto your body's edge. Your grip
Grows firmer, and shall never slip.
The Woman places in our hands her soul,
O Fire. We shall never let it go!

Up from Dust

A Forensic Anthropologist Breaks Bad News
to the Arapaho

The evidence, for me, lies in the pains
Displayed upon their furrowed, worried faces
As I explore the corpse, but find no traces,
Tasked with analyzing the remains.

Hold it together, Doctor, keep your cool.
Here comes the part no scientist enjoys:
"These skeletons are not your missing boys
Exhumed at Richard Henry Indian School."

I feel I lack—like them—the heart, the liver,
Life-granting, vital fluids—bile and gall;
No word of cure nor ceremonial shawl;
Removed, returned, reburied at Wind River.

Villanelle on a Line by Plenty Coups

"The ground on which we stand is sacred ground,"
The blood of those we love—silt, peat, and sand.
For this, we and our children, too, are bound.

If you must probe it, make your dig profound
In order to find Nature's share of land.
The ground on which we stand is sacred ground.

Our forebears fill its surface. Spin around.
Take up a fistful. Sift it from your hand.
For this, we and our children, too, are bound.

With roots to weave their long braids—parched and browned—
By Burnt Lip and Bad War Deed, they are clanned.
The ground on which we stand is sacred ground.

On this, we dance! The drums of sunlight pound,
As their life forces and their love demand.
For this, we and our children, too, are bound.

Where—other than in wind—may they be found?
Our feet leave an impression like a brand.
The ground on which we stand is sacred ground.
For this, we and our children, too, are bound.

At the Museum of the Cherokee Indian

Now having crossed great distances and entered
The room, I clear my throat, and swallow spittle,
To find a tribesman like a mountain, centered,
Supplied with twigs of river cane to whittle.

Behind a folding table clothed in red,
He hunches, carving tool in hand, and scowls,
And bows his glossy, black, bare, heavy head
As though his spirit animals were owls.

Perturbed at worst, unfriendly at the best,
He seems a tribesman there against his will—
In "costume," staged, traditionally dressed,
And slow at work, as though to hide his skill.

I greet him: *Osiyo*, the dialect
Of Western Cherokee—sure in my face
He sees our inbred "pedigrees" connect,
And that my tongue does not speak out of place.

My confidence does not go unrewarded.
My brother recognizes me at once.
This frowning mountain—tacit, placid, guarded—
Pauses from the task at hand, then grunts,

"Si qu'un?"—that inquiry whose English meaning
Is "Things are fine?" *Si qu'un*, I nod, *wado*,
In thanks when he resumes his backward leaning.
Stoic approval speaks, though doesn't show.

Long pause, the grunt—they're dusty ways. And I,
A cherished child, protected from all harms,
Am part of them until the day I die.
My mother's people fold me in their arms.

Remembering How My Native American
Grandfather Told Me a Pregnant Woman
Had Swallowed Watermelon Seeds

> *"You might as well cut a five-year-old child's head off! A
> woman will . . . take the risk of dying with her baby, rather
> than to live without a child."*
>   *—Cherokee Shaman Wili-westi, on learning of the White
> Man's abortion procedures, "Cherokee belief and practice with
> regard to childbirth," Frans M. Olbrechts,* Anthropos, *Jan.–
> Apr. 1931, pg. 19*

The shamans can't contain what they don't know.
Showing such astonishment, they curse.
They call it "murder medicine." *Wado.*[*]

They shame, ". . . for Womanhood would rather go
And die than live without a child to nurse."
The shamans can't contain what they don't know.

While *she* receives a bowl, but *he*, a bow;
While warriors shake scalps, avowed in verse,
They call it "murder medicine." *Wado.*

Into the *osi* menses shack, all flow.
The midwives murmur, "Swallow Shepherd's Purse . . ."
The shamans can't contain what they don't know.

---

*   Wado: Cherokee, meaning "thank you."

Since Suicide Root[†] will keep an embryo
From coming—till the purchase of her hearse—
They call it "murder medicine." *Wado.*

The watermelon seeds inside her grow
Till she becomes taboo—and what is worse?
The shamans can't contain what they don't know.
They call it "murder medicine." *Wado.*

---

†   Cicuta maculata was reputed among the Cherokee to be an oral contraceptive, though discouraged with a social stigma of immorality attached to the woman taking it, and prescribed with a warning that the woman's resulting infertility would be permanent.

Regarding Russell and Remington

For Timothy Murphy

I tell you, Tim—if manly Charlie Russell
And Frederic Remington were still around,
The former, at it with his gaucho muscle—
The latter, at it with his Indian mound—
Each one would lay aside his paints, immerse
His brush in turpentine, pick up your verse,
And, having read one line, would cry, "Astound-
Ing!" Mine? Each man would mouth it as he frowned,
Mind wandering to desert regions cursed
By women trading wampum counterfeit,
And turn aside to brass spittoons, and spit.
Their jaws they'd clench, their booted toes they'd curl,
Pretending not to recognize a *girl*—
To mutter, in those male minds, "Mother Wit!"

Coushatta Scholar

This young man from the land of Gulf Coast plains—
Scholastic grants and stifling student loans
In hand—draws stymied breath and takes great pains
To dress in all the tribal clothes he owns.

Each lettered jacket, every printed tee
Which bears the sovereign "Coushatta" label
He dons, to say, "I am not Cherokee,"
But with as little breath as he is able.

Though, there in Carolina, everywhere
A Native goes, the Trail of Tears will loom
Above him. Like a vapor in the air,
An ever-present, fatalistic fume,

An overhanging, heavy, violet cloud,
It strains the individual's resolve
To bare his tribal merit, to be proud,
Finish with honors, conquer, and evolve.

On Monday, the Coushatta cap is worn.
Then Tuesday comes the short Coushatta shirt,
Laundered endlessly, until it's torn,
Despised and scorned, despite the lack of dirt.

Upon his mother's coming, he will cry
How everyone assumes each Native's face
Is interchangeable with those nearby,
And every tribe is native to *this* place.

Ostenaco

Undoubtedly, the bloody tomahawk
Which we have kept in hand, for so long raised
Against our siblings of this different race,
Must now—and evermore—be deeply buried
Within the soil, never to be lifted
Again, but left forever in the earth.

Whoever shall withdraw it from the earth,
Whoever digs this grisly tomahawk
Contrary to these articles, in lifted
Aggression—let the punishment be raised
Equivalent to their wrongdoing. Buried
This weapon must remain, beneath each race.

Take care of your behavior towards this race,
Whom we must now regard upon the earth
As we regard ourselves, till we are buried
Ourselves, beside the bloody tomahawk—
No more to be brought back to life and raised,
No more to be revitalized and lifted.

Desiring peace, my spirit will be lifted.
Should we neglect to look upon their race
With strict respect, more warfare will be raised.
They have their fill of fighting on the earth.
Ferocious to our foes, this tomahawk—
The symbol of abhorrence—must be buried.

So likewise—let your disrespect be buried,
And hail these warriors, your voices lifted
To those who have endured our tomahawk,
Who venture toward us from the white man's race.
Embed your enmity in Mother Earth,
From whom—these Christians claim—we shall be raised.

Let no dispute, nor one complaint, be raised.
Like tomahawks, let dissonance be buried.
Bellow your safety war songs on the earth,
Heard from a mile away, our prayers lifted,
As toward this peaceable reward we race,
Trusting a benign white tomahawk.

For my ferocious songs, forever lifted—
Emblems of blessing on our brothers' race—
Are my new war tool, my new tomahawk.

Strong Feather's Father

Rise, Daughter, wash your face and be a man;
Splash ruthlessly, erasing every tear.
Then I will introduce you as my son,
And you will have your choice of a career.

When words engulf you, ponder on this day
When you and I conversed, you stilled your lip,
And I advised you: set your dreams aside,
For you cannot afford such scholarship

As has been offered; neither will the sergeant
Recruit you to the war against your will,
With promise to promote you to potential
If you will sign provided lines, and kill.

Rise, Daughter—once my daughter, now my son;
My good-for-nothing girl, become my boy.
Suck up the bitter water pooled before you.
No grief displayed, with even less of joy.

To My Brother-in-Law Studying Indigenous Cuisine

Supportive of your tasteful mission,
Encouraging your ripe ambition,
I send you this authoritative book.
Look upon the Native,

That you fulfill your calling, Jeff,
Becoming an accomplished chef
Sharing our indigenous cuisine,
Gleaning from it, thus.

May it delight. Although you see
Its author is not Cherokee,
Each recipe will whet the appetite.
Bison ribs, dried apple,

Stuffed blossoms of the winter squash,
Prepared with sumac and panache,
Sunflowers served in sage sauté and braised,
Glazed hazelnut sorbet.

The maker, a Lakota Sioux,
With juniper and roast elk stew
Through the use of culinary ash,
Shuns the ordinary.

The flours, made of acorn meal
Or turnips, seem beyond what's real—
Amaranth, which grows beside the road,
Thrown in oil and fried.

Food fantasy, it seems—and yet,
Such customs we must not forget,
But, like our language, keep them on our tongue,
Young, and never sour.

My Mother at Lookout Mountain

This photograph of her within a cave,
Retrieved from trash inside a travel trunk,
Is what I love, and what I have to save.

Her chin is raised, her gaze is dropped but brave,
As though defying how far she has sunk.
This photograph of her within a cave,

This scene—set in a mountain's architrave
To which the Cherokees of old once slunk—
Is what I love, and what I have to save.

Behind the camera, equally as grave,
I see him taking it—her father, Monk—
This photograph of her inside a cave.

Madonna of the Aracoeli nave,
Lost in a world of halo-wanting junk,
Is what I love, and what I have to save.

Its edges warped, to form a crumpled wave
Which heated time and heavy term have shrunk,
This photograph of her within a cave
Is what I love, and what I have to save.

The Native Strain

"We never talk about the Native strain,"
My mother warned in secret, early on.
My father honored her. Our photos—drawn
From generations, gray with filmy grain—

Were never framed and flaunted, on display
Like other people's. Faces by the dozens
Remained in albums—uncles, aunts, and cousins
Enclosed in boxes, shelved and stowed away.

Her father, although handsome, could not pass.
But this fact was as absent from discussion
As crass vernacular, or formal Russian,
Or choruses of mountain man bluegrass.

Our Native ties, however, were the sole
Connections we could talk about at all:
A tightly bound clan, insular and small,
Whose lives we heard as through a locked keyhole.

To read my mother's scrapbooks, one would think
The Indians were our one folk, for none
On our white side received us—they would shun
Us totally, to be our "missing link,"

So they received her mention on no page.
This was Grandmother's lifelong punishment,
Dishonoring her people—wild, hell-bent
On "savages," at fifteen years of age.

No single nor escorted Anglo member
From my maternal grandam's well-heeled kin
Would travel down by train, nor enter in
To my grandfather's house, that I remember.

Occasionally, I might overhear
Some snippet of a whispered conversation
Long-distance—when my wild imagination
Would rampage, and the mystery disappear.

The while Monk drew a breath, I never saw
Those Scots Virginians. Untamed Tennessee
Became an oft-seen, second home to me—
The birthplace of my "alien" papaw

They called "Damned Injun" to Grandmother's face.
On Lover's Leap—the tragic promontory
Where Cherokees maintained the moving story
Of Sautee's and Nacoochee's deaths took place,

The ancient Romeo and Juliet
Of Native America—he loved to stand;
On Lookout Mountain, where he could command
A view of seven states, all in a set;

Where Chickamauga Cherokees defied
Colonial encroachment, and no cragging
Of cliffs is customary—there, where Dragging
Canoe once took the Cherokee to hide.

Those were the photos hung in every room,
Of precipice and mountain, peak and bluff:
High, low, as though there could not be enough,
With scenes of snow, by harvest, or abloom.

Cliff faces were the faces we would see,
The hill, the valley, and the still blue lake:
The earth for whom our forebears would forsake
Their tribe, their culture, and their family.

Some Other Indians

Some other Indians mock me for my love
Of feathers, stones, and for my stilted talk,
And that I stop to watch the circling hawk,
And that I may be stilled by mourning dove
And blue jay both, before me or above.

They whistle shrilly, while they watch me walk
For miles in rain and cold, to pick a stalk
Of tasseled corn, or stamens of foxglove.

But Grandfather growls, "The child is a poet.
Leave her alone, and should she wish to weep
Because the shamans chant, because the birds
Have spoken—though the rest of you don't know it,
This speech of winged things—snicker in your sleep;
For I would rather have oldfangled words."

For the Kickingbirds

Native American prayer on an arrowhead
Hung at the doorway which leads to my library,
Always, your artwork henceforth will inspire me.

When will I see you again, gifted Cherokee?
Gasp at your sculpture, and purchase your pottery?
Speak to you closely, with love, brought from Gatlinburg?

Well I remember that powwow, where you and I
Met, while the jingle-dress girls strode with dignity
Past us, their hands on their hips in solemnity.

Kind but bemused you appeared, as the ritual
Happened beyond us, amid your original
Striped-clay creations, accepting yet skeptical.

Firing your kiln in the Tennessee wilderness,
Etch, for my sake, the bold head of a buffalo.
Sculpt for me, cousins, a wolf with a butterfly.

Tables I see, filled with sages and savages,
Headdresses, feathers, removed from their packages
Gingerly, so the baked clay takes no breakages.

Fingers I see, your skilled hands moving merchandise
Here to there, transferring statues with eagle eyes,
Deft and astute as professional artisans.

Obviously at a loss—for the craftsmanship
Stuns me, the five clays combined, the streaked media
Blended and carved with such cunning—I sing of it!

Young Althea

Young Althea—where is the ground you wanted?
Growing lonely? Sociable near the bedding,
Double ruffled, lavender blossoms spreading
Over the lily?

Never, never say I displaced you cruelly,
Crying, "Crazy stock!" in a storm of bias,
"Stand in banished countryside!" glib and pious . . .
Level or hilly?

Rose of Sharon—Grandmother's orchard umbrage—
East or west? Or waving at Choctaw neighbors?
Lead me there, before I begin my labors,
Lest I look silly,

Planting you discordant to dusty custom,
Rooting you in doom, to defy your habit,
Dying rudely, midway from dove and rabbit—
Cheated and chilly.

The Cranes on Black Mulch Isle

Late in the evening, night appearing soon,
We plant white phlox and violet in the ground
Before the storms arrive, the sparrows' sound
Replaced by haunting mourning dove and loon.

A lifeless alligator opens great
But harmless jaws before me, bared in vain
His teeth toward a graceful female crane
Beside her mate—placed there by my own mate.

This April moon endows my spouse's labors
Of love for me with mystical effect,
As flying, biting bugs—blood to collect—
Accost us, who outstay retiring neighbors.

Oasis he has made for me. The black
Mulch shifting underneath us, like the sands
Of Colorado through Comanche hands,
Has bowed his spirit, with his breaking back.

It's said the skilled Comanche hands could fire
One arrow, and before that first would sink
To earth, could send five more without a blink—
And, standing here, I realize my desire.

May I attain—like my outmoded kin
Who stood their filched, consanguine ground to shoot—
The skill and power which might execute
Five piercing points, before my first sinks in.

Massachusetts's Mother

Plymouth, 1620

When last the glorious light of all the sky
Below the globe was gone, when birds will close
Their throats, then I began to rest, as my
Routine of habit is, to take repose.
Before the moment my tired eyes had tightened,
I saw an apparition, so I thought,
At which my spirit was extremely frightened,
And trembled, witnessing this sight. Distraught,
"My son, whom I have loved!" a phantom wept,
"Behold the one who nursed you, she who fed
You, warmed you, watched you while you slept.
These immigrants who desecrate the dead,
These savage thieves who harm our noble race,
Who treat our ancient customs with disdain,
Who came with hateful manner to deface
My burial place—your mother must complain,
Imploring your assistance to oppose
And take revenge against this alien nation,
Or otherwise, my eyes shall never close
In rest, in my eternal habitation."

From Chilhowee Mountain

When I look out from proud Chilhowee Mountain,
Upon a boulder balanced on the ground,
Subdued, I hear two crows call, with the sound
The rushing river utters like a fountain
Of voices lost and waiting, once more found.
I raise one hand to shade my eyes, no doubting
My deepest intuition, all around
Me nothing but the russet leaves and browned,
Snug fringe of my attire as I stand scouting
The landscape from nine hundred feet in air.
The boulder is a soul beneath me, shouting,
Reminding me of my ancestral birth
Around this mound they call Spearfinger's lair.
No bond exists to rival ours, on earth.

To the Snakeskin on My Path

May I not meet this coming summer
    The form from which your scales are shed
On this machine-laid, man-made pavement
    Shyer creatures shun with dread.

I lasso you, with loops of plastic,
    To burn upon my urban drive,
Bringing a needed springtime shower—
    Your body elsewhere left alive.

Black Back, Pale Belly, subtly shimmer,
    Allowing me to learn that song
Snakes taught the hunter's lips to utter,
    That they might never do him wrong.

Tracking Creator

You cannot trip seditiously behind,
And must—to trek with Him—stay on your feet,
Not shrinking in rebellion, disinclined,
Nor false and bitter, settling in your seat.

You must keep moving, moving every moment,
Lest you lose sight, in indecision wallow,
Your private trails replacing His bestowment.
His edict isn't "Find your way," but "Follow."

Reservation

My reservation is a reservation
Where Red Paint gazes at his mobile phone—
A transcendental Indian, alone
Adorned in the full feather of our Nation;
While Wildcatt emulates his isolation,
Around his throat, a choker made of bone—
Suspicious, steady, ready to disown
His flesh and blood, with no clear explanation.
Along Main Avenue, they greet the tourists
Who hold a honeymooning hand and laugh,
Who claim, "We share your shame. We share your grief."
But Wildcatt and Red Paint—grim as jurists—
Arise to pose for one more photograph,
And only their sad eyes show disbelief.

Jennifer Reeser is the author of six collections of poetry, most recently, *Strong Feather* (Able Muse Press, 2022), and preceding it, *Indigenous* (Able Muse Press, 2019), which was awarded Best Poetry Book of 2019 by *Englewood Review of Books*. Her first, *An Alabaster Flask*, was the winner of the Word Press First Book Prize. X. J. Kennedy wrote that her debut "ought to have been a candidate for a Pulitzer." Her  third, *Sonnets from the Dark Lady and Other Poems*, was a finalist for the Donald Justice Prize. Her fourth, *The Lalaurie Horror*, debuted as an Amazon bestseller in the category of Epic Poetry. Reeser's poems, reviews, and translations of Russian, French, Cherokee and other Native American languages have appeared in *Poetry, Rattle*, the *Hudson Review, Recours au Poème, Light Quarterly*, the *Formalist*, the *Dark Horse, SALT, Able Muse*, and elsewhere.

A biracial writer of European American and Native American Indian ancestry, Reeser was born in Louisiana. She studied English at college in Oklahoma and also at McNeese State University in Louisiana. She now divides her time between the Louisiana Gulf Coast and her land on the Cherokee Reservation in Indian Country near Tahlequah, Oklahoma, capital of the Cherokee Nation of which her family is a part.

ALSO FROM ABLE MUSE PRESS

Jacob M. Appel, *The Cynic in Extremis: Poems*

William Baer, *Times Square and Other Stories; New Jersey Noir: A Novel;*
 New Jersey Noir (Cape May): A Novel; New Jersey Noir (Barnegat Light): A Novel

Lee Harlin Bahan, *A Year of Mourning (Petrarch): Translation*

Melissa Balmain, *Walking in on People (Able Muse Book Award for Poetry)*

Ben Berman, *Strange Borderlands: Poems; Figuring in the Figure: Poems;*
 Writing While Parenting: Essays

David Berman, *Progressions of the Mind: Poems*

Lorna Knowles Blake, *Green Hill (Able Muse Book Award for Poetry)*

Michael Cantor, *Life in the Second Circle: Poems*

Catherine Chandler, *Lines of Flight: Poems*

William Conelly, *Uncontested Grounds: Poems*

Maryann Corbett, *Credo for the Checkout Line in Winter: Poems;*
 Street View: Poems; In Code: Poems

Will Cordeiro, *Trap Street (Able Muse Book Award for Poetry)*

Brian Culhane, *Remembering Lethe: Poems*

John Philip Drury, *Sea Level Rising: Poems*

Rhina P. Espaillat, *And After All: Poems*

Anna M. Evans, *Under Dark Waters: Surviving the* Titanic*: Poems*

Nicole Caruso Garcia, *Oxblood: Poems*

Stephen Gibson, *Frida Kahlo in Fort Lauderdale: Poems*

D. R. Goodman, *Greed: A Confession: Poems*

Carrie Green, *Studies of Familiar Birds: Poems*

Margaret Ann Griffiths, *Grasshopper: The Poetry of M A Griffiths*

Janis Harrington, *How to Cut a Woman in Half: Poems*

Katie Hartsock, *Bed of Impatiens: Poems; Wolf Trees: Poems*

Elise Hempel, *Second Rain: Poems*

Jan D. Hodge, *Taking Shape: Carmina figurata;*
 The Bard & Scheherazade Keep Company: Poems

Ellen Kaufman, *House Music: Poems; Double-Parked, with Tosca: Poems*

Len Krisak, *Say What You Will (Able Muse Book Award for Poetry)*

Emily Leithauser, *The Borrowed World (Able Muse Book Award for Poetry)*

Hailey Leithauser, *Saint Worm: Poems*

Carol Light, *Heaven from Steam: Poems*

Kate Light, *Character Shoes: Poems*

April Lindner, *This Bed Our Bodies Shaped: Poems*

Martin McGovern, *Bad Fame: Poems*

Jeredith Merrin, *Cup: Poems*

Richard Moore, *Selected Poems;*
    The Rule That Liberates: An Expanded Edition: Selected Essays

Richard Newman, *All the Wasted Beauty of the World: Poems*

Alfred Nicol, *Animal Psalms: Poems*

Deirdre O'Connor, *The Cupped Field (Able Muse Book Award for Poetry)*

Frank Osen, *Virtue, Big as Sin (Able Muse Book Award for Poetry)*

Alexander Pepple (Editor), *Able Muse Anthology;*
    Able Muse: A Review of Poetry, Prose & Art (semiannual, winter 2010 on)

James Pollock, *Sailing to Babylon: Poems*

Aaron Poochigian, *The Cosmic Purr: Poems; Manhattanite (Able Muse Book Award for Poetry)*

Tatiana Forero Puerta, *Cleaning the Ghost Room: Poems*

Jennifer Reeser, *Indigenous: Poems; Strong Feather: Poems*

John Ridland, *Sir Gawain and the Green Knight (Anonymous): Translation;*
    Pearl (Anonymous): Translation

Kelly Rowe, *Rise above the River (Able Muse Book Award for Poetry)*

Stephen Scaer, *Pumpkin Chucking: Poems*

Hollis Seamon, *Corporeality: Stories*

Ed Shacklee, *The Blind Loon: A Bestiary*

Carrie Shipers, *Cause for Concern (Able Muse Book Award for Poetry)*

Matthew Buckley Smith, *Dirge for an Imaginary World (Able Muse Book Award for Poetry)*

Susan de Sola, *Frozen Charlotte: Poems*

Barbara Ellen Sorensen, *Compositions of the Dead Playing Flutes: Poems*

Rebecca Starks, *Time Is Always Now: Poems; Fetch, Muse: Poems*

Sally Thomas, *Motherland: Poems*

Paulette Demers Turco (Editor), *The Powow River Poets Anthology II*

Rosemerry Wahtola Trommer, *Naked for Tea: Poems*

Wendy Videlock, *Wise to the West: Poems; Slingshots and Love Plums: Poems;*
    The Dark Gnu and Other Poems; Nevertheless: Poems

Richard Wakefield, *A Vertical Mile: Poems; Terminal Park: Poems*

Gail White, *Asperity Street: Poems*

Chelsea Woodard, *Vellum: Poems*

Rob Wright, *Last Wishes: Poems*

www.ablemusepress.com